JOURNAL

PETER PAUPER PRESS, INC.
WHITE PLAINS, NEW YORK

PETER PAUPER PRESS
Fine Books and Gifts Since 1928

Our Company

In 1928, at the age of twenty-two, Peter Beilenson began printing books on a small press in the basement of his parents' home in Larchmont, New York. Peter—and later his wife, Edna—sought to create fine books that sold at "prices even a pauper could afford."

Today, still family owned and operated, Peter Pauper Press continues to honor our founders' legacy—and our customers' expectations—of beauty, quality, and value.

Cover art: The LuEsther T. Mertz Library, New York Botanical Garden / Art Resource, New York. A colored woodcut by Hiroshige II Utagawa of cherry blossoms viewing (Japanese garden prints).

Designed by David Cole Wheeler

Copyright © 2012
Peter Pauper Press, Inc.
202 Mamaroneck Avenue
White Plains, NY 10601
All rights reserved
ISBN 978-1-4413-1037-8
Printed in China
7 6

Visit us at www.peterpauper.com